Ways to Pay for Long-Term Care

This reference guide is based
on excerpts from the best selling books,
*The Arizona Medicaid and
Veterans Pension Guide*
&
Medicaid For Millionaires

Bonus:
*Secrets that Arizona Medicaid
and The VA doesn't want you to know!*

A Compassionate & Devoted Memory Care Community

At Mosaic Gardens at Scottsdale, we prioritize providing exceptional living experiences for our residents and their families. Our commitment to quality is reflected in our array of amenities.

- ✳ Customized Care
- ✳ Prioritizing the needs and happiness of each resident
- ✳ Help to and from meals and activities.
- ✳ Creating a warm, loving environment for residents
- ✳ Encouraging engagement in day-to-day activities
- ✳ Inviting amenities

SEE OUR BROCHURE

Schedule a Tour Today
480-769-8201
sales1@MosaicgGardensScottsdale.com

WHAT WE DO
Unmatched Person-Centered Care

Mosaic Gardens at Scottsdale is committed to attending to our residents with compassion and respect while always considering their personal preferences.

- 24-hour On-site Care Staff
- Licensed Nurse on Staff
- Eating Aid Services
- Dressing & Grooming
- Walking Aid Services
- Bathing & Toileting
- Walking Aid Services

- Areas for Socialization
- Medication Management
- Housekeeping
- Daily Team-Led Activities
- Religious Services
- Scheduled Transportation
- Health & Exercise Programs

Learn more about our wonderful and caring community.
Call us today at 480-769-8201
MosaicGardensmc.com

Long-Term Care Planning Services Provided by:

Steve Dabbs, CMP™, AIF® and VA Accredited Claims Agent
Certified Medicaid Planner™
Accredited Investment Fiduciary®

Steve Bragg, VP
Vice President
Client Support & Communication

- Long-Term Care Wealth Management
  - Long-Term Care Risk Planning
  - Income Planning to Manage Ongoing Care Costs
  - Long-Term Care Wealth Management

- Long-Term Care Insurance Planning
  - Traditional Long-Term Care Insurance Plans
  - Hybrid Asset Based Long-Term Care Insurance
  - Short-Term Care Insurance Plans

- Medicaid Planning
  - Medicaid Crisis & Non-Crisis Planning

- Veterans Long-Term Care Benefits Planning
  - Veterans Pension

Cecilia Dabbs, CMP™, CLDP
Certified Medicaid Planner™
Certified Legal Document Preparer

- Long-Term Care Legal Document Preparation
  - Income Only Trusts, a.k.a Miller Trust
  - Power of Attorney Package
  - Medicaid Planning Trust Preparation
  - VA Asset Protection Trust Preparation
  - Last Will and Testament
  - Living Trusts

My team and I would love to speak at your church, club or association.

We will provide my book "Ways to Pay for Long-Term Care," at no charge to those who attended.

Call Steve Dabbs at 480-967-8477 to set your meeting up.

SCAN ME

Need a radio or TV guest?

America's long-term care crisis is real and upon us.

Help me get the word out.
Call to schedule me for your next show.

Steve did a wonderful job for us, everything was settled fast, his knowledge of working with ALTCS was amazing. There is no way I could have completed this without him. I have already recommended his services to other friends who have need of his services. So very grateful for his help!

★ ★ ★ ★ ★

Judy K.

I have never had someone work so diligently to help me. This was the most frustrating process I have ever been through, but Steve and Cecilia did not give up. They went the extra mile, and I am eternally grateful. I highly recommend them!!

★ ★ ★ ★ ★

Julie D.

Steve's knowledge of funding solutions opens doors for individuals and makes them aware of options they would not have known otherwise. Steve puts the interests of his clients first and educates them as he goes so that they are ultimately better advocates for themselves and their loved ones.

★ ★ ★ ★ ★

Sandy D.

"Ways to Pay for Long-Term Care" contains excerpts from the book, The Arizona Medicaid and Veterans Pension Guide and Medicaid For Millionaires. Here is what the experts say about the author, Steve Dabbs.

The Arizona Medicaid and Veterans Pension Guide

Book Reviews

Michael Anthony, JD, CMP™

Congratulations to Steve Dabbs for completing his book on Arizona Medicaid and Veterans' Pension benefits.

"Steve is the best Medicaid Planner in Arizona." His book is insightful and helpful for anyone facing long-term care issues. He takes a very complicated subject matter and makes it easy to understand. I hope you enjoy reading it as much as I did.

Michael Anthony, JD, CMP™ | A Certified Medicaid Planner™ and the author of the largest print book on Medicaid/Medi-Cal Planning, "The Medicaid Planning Guidebook," used by Medicaid Planners all over the United States.

Printed in the United States of America

Author Steve M. Dabbs
Tempe, Arizona 85283
info@carefundingsolutions.com

480-967-8477

www.CareFundingSolutions.com
www.VeteransPension.com
www.ALTCS.org
www.ArizonaMedicaid.com
www.MedicaidforMillionaires.com

Ordering Information:
Quantity sales. Special discounts are available on quantity purchases by corporations, associations, assisted living communities, and others. For details, contact the "Book Sales Department" at the address above.

"The 2024 Arizona Medicaid and Veterans Pension Summary Guide"
This reduced reference guide is based on excerpts from the Best Seller, "The Arizona Medicaid and Veterans Pension Guide." / Steve M. Dabbs — 1st 2024

ISBN: 9798340713889 (Mosaic Gardens Memory Care at Scottsdale Edition)

TABLE OF CONTENTS

PREFACE

Chronic diseases are conditions that last one year or more, causing the need for long-term care or extended care. This is due to ongoing medical care and affects a person's ability to perform or limit activities of daily living or ADLs, which causes the need for long-term care or extended care.

Long-term or extended care has caused the loss of life savings to millions of retired individuals, robbing them of the lifestyle they once enjoyed, often leaving them penniless and their heirs with nothing.

The need for long-term care could be responsible for taking your dignity, independence, and pride in your retirement years.

A needless financial tragedy and one that is avoidable!

The need for long-term care is the worst financial problem that seniors and Baby Boomers face today, and to make matters worse, costs are rising as much as twice that of the national inflation rate.

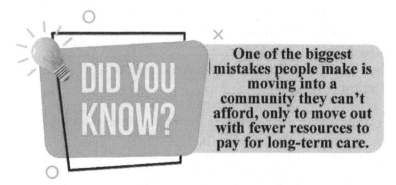

DID YOU KNOW? One of the biggest mistakes people make is moving into a community they can't afford, only to move out with fewer resources to pay for long-term care.

Long-term care planning is essential to avoid making the same mistake.

Remember, you must act on the information and strategies to benefit.

Without action, there is only a reaction!

ABOUT THE AUTHOR

STEVE M. DABBS, CMP™, AIF®, CEP®, CLTC®

Vietnam Veteran
Financial Planner/Investment Advisor
Certified Long-Term Care Specialist™
Certified Estate Planner™
VA Accredited Claims Agent -
    Accredited by the Department of Veterans Affairs
Certified Medicaid Planner™
Accredited Investment Fiduciary®
Member "National Guardianship Association"
Non-Fiction Author

Steve Dabbs began his working career in the Navy and is a Vietnam veteran, serving on the USS Racine LST-1191.

He entered the financial services industry in 1978. He has been an Investment Advisor Representative since 2011. In 2018 he started "LTC Wealth Management, LLC," a Registered Investment Advisory firm. Dabbs founded the firm with a focus on Long-Term Care Financial Planning.

In 2003, he began helping veterans by educating them on the Veterans Pension with Aid and Attendance benefit program.

Then, on June 30, 2011, he became a VA-Accredited Claims Agent accredited by the Department of Veterans Affairs.

As a VA-Accredited Claims Agent, I can legally represent a veteran before the Department of Veterans Affairs in preparing, presenting, and prosecuting VA claims.

On August 1, 2012, Dabbs became a Certified for Long-Term Care® - CLTC®.

Then, in 2016, he became a Certified Medicaid Planner™, CMP™. To achieve certification, a CMP™ must meet specific education and experience requirements and show proficiency in Medicaid Planning or ALTCS Planning in Arizona.

The fact that the VA accredits Steve Dabbs and a CMP™ demonstrates that Dabbs has a solid working knowledge of how the VA Pension program works with Medicaid/ ALTCS and how they conflict.

In 2018, he became an Accredited Investment Fiduciary®, putting Dabbs above the pack. The Accredited Investment Fiduciary® (AIF®) is an ethical certification issued by Fi360.

As a fiduciary, Steve Dabbs is required by law to put a client's best interest first.

Today he is a national mentor, trainer, and consultant on Medicaid/ALTCS planning and Veterans Pension with Aid and Attendance benefits, actively advising financial planners and attorneys throughout the United States.

And now Steve Dabbs, the Author.

AIF- Fiduciary

Contact Steve Dabbs

What is a CMP?

MY WHY

Steve Dabbs, CMP™, AIF®,
VA Accredited Claims Agent
Certified Medicaid Planner™
Accredited Investment Fiduciary®

It was a beautiful day in the spring of 2004. I was to speak on a little-known benefit called "The Veterans Improved Pension with Aid and Attendance[1]."

In 2004 few veterans were aware of this veteran's long-term care benefit.

Once I finished the presentation, a lady asked, "Can I ask you a question?"

I love to joke with people. I responded, "I'm married if that is your question!" She laughed and said, "No, that's not my question." She continued, explaining, "I recently lost my husband, and we spent all our money caring for him. I now have $25,000 to live on for the rest of my life, is there any way I can go back in time and get these benefits?"

As I looked into her eyes, I saw her sadness and fear. It was the look of fear of running out of money.

I had to say, "No, there isn't, ma'am. I'm sorry."

From that day forward I vowed to do everything I could to prevent this from being someone else's story.

INTRODUCTION

Ways to Pay For Long-Term Care

The What, Who, Why, When, Where, and How to Pay for It?

What is Long-Term Care?

Long-term care includes both help with Activities of Daily Living; ADLs, and Incidental Activities of Daily Living; IADLS.

Activities of Daily Living or ADLs include eating, bathing, grooming, dressing, transferring, mobility, toileting, and hygiene.

Incidental Activities of Daily Living include shopping, food preparation, housekeeping, laundering, managing finances, medication assistance, using the telephone, and transportation.

Who Needs Long-Term Care?

Anybody unable to perform everyday functions or activities that a healthy or unimpaired person can do without help may need long-term care services. There is no specific age range for those who benefit from these services, but most individuals are over age 65.

Why Consider Long-Term Care?

Aging is the leading cause of the need for long-term care. Over 70% of those over 65 will need long-term care for at least a two-year period.

When Will You Need Long-Term Care?

The need for long-term care can happen at any time to anybody. It can be a gradual progression over time due to aging or happen suddenly due to an accident or stroke.

Where to Seek Long-Term Care?

Most of the time, family members are the first care providers.

After a family caregiver can no longer provide the level of care needed, where to go for care?

What Are the Steps?

First, know you have a need and accept your need for care.

Second, seek advice. Contact a Senior Placement Specialist.

Third, choose a place that will best fit your personal needs.

Fourth, organize your finances and know what you can afford before moving. Understand and utilize all of the various care funding solutions. Here's where a Certified Medicaid Planner help.

Fifth, after you have chosen a place, check the Arizona Department of Health Services website for enforcement actions against the care provider or assisted living. See azfhs.gov

The Perfect Storm

In recent years, the cost of long-term care has been dramatically affected by inflation in the United States.

The cost increases in the long-term care industry are nearly double that of the national inflation rate, with no end in sight.

To make matters even worse for those needing long-term care. There is a caregiver shortage in the United States.

These issues have made long-term care planning essential to any financial plan. Unfortunately, most planners do not know how to do this type of wealth management. I founded LTC Wealth Management to address the need for this type of planning.

SECTION I

WHAT IS EXTENDED CARE OR LONG-TERM CARE?

HOW TO FIND THE RIGHT CARE?

HOME CARE

ADULT CARE

ASSISTED LIVING

NURSING HOME

Chapter One

WHAT'S LONG-TERM CARE OR EXTENDED CARE?

Long-Term Care or Extended Care is special assistance with activities of daily living or ADLs.

Long-term care is often needed because of an illness, injury, disability, or cognitive impairment. Care can be in a nursing home, assisted living community, home care, home health care, or community-based care by a family member.

Extended care services range from help with day-to-day activities, such as assistance with:

- Bathing
- Dressing
- Toileting – getting up and down and hygiene
- Continence care
- Transferring – in or out of bed or chair
- Eating / Feeding – cutting up food if a choking risk
- Cognitive impairment assistance (Alzheimer's or Dementia)
- Mobility
- Grooming

What are the Chances this Will Happen to You?

More than two out of three people in the United States will be caregivers or care receivers!

Long-Term Care is a Serious Matter

In Fact: 70% of all Americans are expected to need long-term care at some point in their lives. (National Academy of Elder Law Attorneys)

For a couple turning 65, there is a 75% chance that one of them will need long-term care. (The Wall Street Journal)

Over 70% of people with Alzheimer's live at home and receive 75% of the assistance they need from unpaid caregivers. (Understanding Alzheimer's, Alzheimer's Association)

The average annual cost of a private room in a nursing home in Arizona was $109,026 in 2022 and is expected to jump to over $191,000 by 2040. (Genworth – Annual Cost survey)

63% of caregivers use their own retirement and savings funds to pay for care for another person. (Genworth – Beyond Dollars 2018)

Conclusion

What are your reasons for not addressing the long-term care issue for you and your loved ones? What are your "denials" and "excuses?"

Do you really want your kids cleaning you and helping you off the toilet?

Do you want your son or daughter lifting you out of the bathtub?

Do you want to lose your dignity?

Do you want the government or nursing home taking your family's inheritance?

I know the thought of this is a little depressing.

However, there are solutions to the problem of long-term care.

Please read on. There are answers to the long-term care financial dilemma.

Chapter Two

WHAT IS A PLACEMENT AGENT?

Should you seek professional help to find the perfect place?

Many start this journey of finding long-term care services without professional help.

The search for the right place can take a lot of time; it can be complicated and confusing. Many looking for care are just handed a list of care homes and communities and expected, with no experience, to find and negotiate the arrangements.

This often causes many to move to an assisted living provider only to learn that their chosen place will not be a good fit, forcing them to have to move again.

Noteworthy: Moving from place to place is unhealthy and should be minimized for the health of the person needing care.

This is why many turn to senior placement agents for help.

What is a Placement Agent?

A placement agent knows the local assisted living homes and communities. Then, based on the level of care, the location, the amenities desired, and the budget, we will recommend the best fit for you or your loved ones' needs.

Best of all, the placement agent is paid by the assisted living care home or community, so this is a "free" service to you.

Need help finding a Placement Agent? Call 855-827-3674.

Chapter Three

HOME CARE VS HOME HEALTH CARE

"Home Care" and "Home Health Care" have similar names but are different types of care services. To fully understand Home Care versus Home Health Care, here are the key differences:

Home Care

Home care provides "non-clinical" or "non-skilled" care.

Caregivers are not licensed but are trained to help with the assistance of activities of daily living.

Daily living activities include bathing, dressing, grooming, cooking, cleaning, transportation, and companionship.

Home care provides care in the home and in assisted living.

Home care can make it possible to stay in your home without going to assisted living.

Home Health Care

Licensed professionals provide home health care, both "clinical" and "skilled" care.

Home health care services are medically related. Home health care professionals can help with things like bathing, grooming, and dressing, but generally only until you can safely do them with the help of a non-skilled caregiver.

Home health care continues as long as your doctor certifies the need for this higher level of care.

Medicare, Medicaid, and most private insurance pay for eligible patients' care within plan limits.

Patients can receive home health care in their residences, assisted living communities, and group homes.

If you need help finding a home care or home health care agency, go to www.CareFundingSolutions.com/stay-home

Chapter Four

HOSPICE AND PALLIATIVE CARE

Hospice Care and Palliative Care are not the same.

What Is Hospice Care?

Hospice Care focuses on the comfort and quality of life of a person with a terminal illness, attending to their emotional and spiritual needs.

To receive Hospice Care, a patient must stop life-prolonging medical treatments. They do so because the side effects outweigh the benefits.

Hospice Care prioritizes comfort and quality of life by reducing pain and suffering.

What does it mean when you are in Hospice Care?

Hospice Care is for people who are nearing the end of their lives. Some also call it "End-of-Life" Care. It includes physical, emotional, social, and spiritual support.

Hospice doesn't always mean death and loss of hope.

Many people still live much longer than six months. Some even live for years after their diagnosis.

You can also stop and restart Hospice Care anytime if you feel that you wish to continue treatment again.

What Is Palliative Care?

On the other hand, Palliative Care helps people with serious illnesses to feel better by preventing or treating their symptoms and side effects.

Palliative care is specialized care aimed at relieving pain and helping people feel better.

SECTION II

WAYS TO PAY FOR EXTENDED CARE

Ways to Pay For Extended Care:

- You pay with your current income and life savings and other assets
- You ask a family member or friend to pay for care
- Funds from a reverse mortgage
- Long-Term Care Insurance
- Use your life insurance -otherwise known as Life Settlements
- Arizona Long-Term Care System (ALTCS), which is Arizona's Medicaid Long-Term Care Insurance benefit program.
- Veterans Pension Benefits, a.k.a Aid and Attendance

Ways To Pay For Long-Term Care

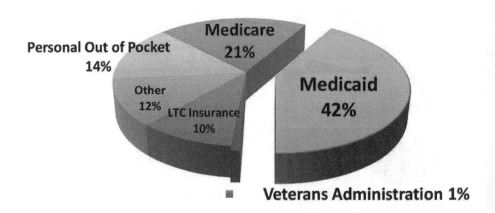

Let's discuss each payment option.

16

Chapter Five

PRIVATE PAY FOR CARE PAY WITH YOUR INCOME AND PERSONAL FUNDS

Fourteen percent of those in the United States use their current income to pay for long-term care, including life savings, home sale proceeds, and other assets. ¥

Some turn to family and friends to help pay for care.

Consider this:

By 2029, 54% of seniors in the middle class will not have the means to pay privately for needed care.**

If married, paying for long-term care could leave spouses without sufficient funds to live for the rest of their lives.

What is Long-Term Care Financial Planning?

Long-term care wealth management is a relatively new type of wealth management platform.

Few financial planners fully understand how the need for care can devastate someone's net worth.

This is why I saw the need to set up LTC Wealth Management, LLC as a fee-based only platform.

Through this platform, I help set realistic expectations for paying for long-term care based on the level of care now and the projected future care costs.

Setting up a steady flow of tax-efficient income to pay for care and, at the same time, utilizing governmental benefits like Medicaid or ALTCS and Veterans Pension benefits.

Accredited Investment Fiduciary®

I have been a financial advisor for over 35 years and am an Accredited Investment Fiduciary. As a fiduciary, I must put the best interest of my clients first in all that I do.

Ask yourself this, "Is your current advisor a "salesperson" or an advisor with your best interest in mind?

(¥) It is noteworthy that less than 5% of the US population over 65 has a net worth of $1 Million.
(Source: US Census Bureau, Survey of Income and Program.)

**2019 study by Caroline F. Pearson, Charlene C. Quinn, Sai Loganathan, A. Rupa Datta, Beth Burnham Mace, and David C. Grabowskian, aging researchers at NORC, a nonpartisan research organization based at the University of Chicago.

Chapter Six

REVERSE MORTGAGE

A Reverse Mortgage is designed to give you access to your home equity without making monthly payments to service the loan.

Instead, you receive a tax-free loan that will not affect your Social Security or Medicare benefits and that you do not have to pay back until you sell your home.

You can choose any combination of these flexible payout options when you get your Reverse Mortgage:

- ➢ A lump sum to cover large expenses
- ➢ Monthly installments to supplement income
- ➢ A line of credit to draw on as needed
- ➢ A combination of the above

In fact, 77% of seniors prefer to stay in their homes, according to a 2021 AARP study. A Reverse Mortgage may be just the program that can make that happen.

You only need to be 62 or older and have sufficient home equity to qualify.

If you want more information on a reverse mortgage and to see if it makes sense to consider this option, call my office.

Chapter Seven

MEDICARE INSURANCE COVERS EXTENDED CARE – RIGHT?

As a Certified Medicaid Planner, I often cringe when I hear Medicare pays for long-term care.

"It Does Not!"

What Is Medicare?

Medicare is a federal program that provides medical coverage to two groups of American citizens. So, who is eligible for Medicare?

Individuals aged 65 and older and people with specific disabilities.

How Much Will Medicare Pay for Long-Term Care?

Some wrongly believe that Medicare also covers long-term care after hospitalization or otherwise. They are wrong. Medicare's long-term care coverage is minimal and only for a short period of time.

See pages 28 and 52 in the "Medicare & You 2024" guidebook.

Medicare doesn't pay for long-term care!

Long-term care includes services that fulfill personal care needs. Long-term care is not always medical-related. It also includes bathing, dressing, feeding, taking care of the beneficiary's hygiene, and helping with a person's daily living activities.

Again, Medicare doesn't cover custodial care (long-term care). Instead, the program provides limited skilled nursing care.

Skilled Nursing Care: Medicare will only pay for the costs of skilled nursing care for the first 20 days, after a minimum of a 3-day hospital stay (midnight stays). After the initial period, the individual has to contribute around $185 per day (2021) toward coinsurance. Medicare will cease to pay for skilled nursing care after 100 days.

Home Health Care: Medicare pays for certain skilled care services to individuals who are homebound due to injury or illness. The doctor treating the individual must agree that skilled care (therapy, nurses, etc.) is required. Here too, the contribution of Medicare is limited. The program will pay for only 28 hours of skilled care per week.

Hospice: The program pays for hospice care for terminally ill patients. For Medicare to cover hospice services, the doctor must provide a certificate that the individual might not live longer than six months. To extend the coverage after six months, the doctor must certify the patient is still terminally ill.

See Short-Term Care Insurance:
https://carefundingsolutions.com/short-term/

 You may like to know that even if you are in an independent living community and under age 85, you may still qualify for a "Short Term Care Plan."

Chapter Eight

LONG-TERM CARE INSURANCE – WHAT'S NEW?

Long-term care insurance helps pay for the services associated with personal and custodial care or activities of daily living (ADLs).

It covers care services in various settings, including nursing homes, assisted living homes, communities, and **in-home care services**.

Long-term care insurance also covers care coordination, cooking, bathing, dressing, eating, and medication management.

By 2030, all baby boomers will be 65 or older. This tsunami of people turning 65 has strained government long-term care programs like Medicaid – ALTCS and Veterans Pension benefits.

This strain on governmental benefits has made whether or not to own long-term care insurance one of the most important financial decision you will need to make.

Why Should You Consider Long-Term Care Insurance?

More than anything, long-term care policy offers peace of mind.

Comparing the Risk:

Life insurance: 100% of us will die at some point, so the need for life insurance is self-evident.

Health insurance: Unless you are incredibly unusual or extremely wealthy, you will need health insurance coverage.

Automobile insurance: One out of every 240 people will have an auto accident and need auto insurance protection. Loan companies require that you have auto insurance to protect your care.

House fire insurance: one in every 1,200 homes will experience a fire. Mortgage companies require fire insurance to protect your home.

One in Two People Will Need Long-Term Care!
Even though long-term care poses the greatest risk of any of the above, nobody is going to make you buy it.

You must purchase this type of insurance on your own.

Who Should Consider Long-Term Care Insurance and Who Should Not?

If you are sandwiched between the extremely rich and poor, then long-term care insurance is the best option for paying for care.

Who Needs Long-Term Care Insurance?

People with an average to above-average net worth should consider long-term care insurance.

Most people prefer not to depend on their children and family for physical help as they become too frail to perform specific ADLs.

Expenses for long-term care services can quickly wipe out your savings in no time, leaving behind unpaid bills and an eviction notice!

How Much Does Long-Term Care Insurance Cost?

The cost of the policy varies from one insurance provider to another.

How much you'll pay also depends on factors such as:

- Your age at the time of purchasing the long-term care insurance policy.
- The coverage and the benefits you need.
- The type of long-term care policy you choose.
- Your health

Keep this in mind:

"You can write a little check to an insurance company now or write a big check to an assisted living community later!"

When Should You Buy Long-Term Care Insurance?

Those who wait too long to purchase a long-term care insurance policy will face high premiums. Some become ineligible due to a pre-existing medical condition, so don't wait until it is too late.

The other extreme of buying too early has some drawbacks. When purchasing too early, the policyholder has to pay premiums for a long time before becoming eligible to receive benefits.

Is there a best age to buy long-term care insurance?

According to The American Association for Long-Term Care Insurance, the sweet spot – the ideal time to buy long-term care insurance – is in a person's mid-50s to early 60s.

Many experts second this recommendation even though most claims occur when the policyholders are in their 70s, 80s, or even 90s.

Roughly 23% of all applications of people in their 60s are denied by insurance companies. This is nearly double the policy applications denied to people in their 50s.

Should you consider short-term care insurance?

If you are over 65 and under age 85, a Short-Term Care program may be a smart alternative to long-term care insurance.

Qualifying for a short-term care insurance program is much easier than long-term care coverage.

In fact, I have often used this type of coverage when someone has been turned down for traditional long-term care insurance. Or the cost is prohibited due to age or health history.

What Are the Different Types of Long-Term Care Insurance?

People looking for long-term care insurance now have more choices than ever. That said, long-term care insurance can be broadly classified into two main types.

Traditional Long-Term Care Insurance (LTCI)

Today most traditional LTCI policies cover nursing home and in-home care services.

Some policies allow you to include additional benefits such as coverage for home modifications, allowing a family member to provide in-home care, or hiring a care manager.

Premiums are paid monthly or annually; some policies offer a waiver of premium once coverage is approved for care.

The actual benefits are paid based on the coverage you choose.

Cash Benefits Policy: The Company will pay the full daily benefits, and you need not show proof of care services received.

Indemnity Policy: The Company will pay the daily benefit upon proof that at least one care service was received per day.

Reimbursement Policy: You submit receipts or other documents proving you paid for care services out-of-pocket, and the company will reimburse you up to the maximum daily benefit limit.

Modern Asset-Based Long-Term Care Insurance

Asset-based long-term care insurance is fast gaining popularity because of the flexibility it offers. Some also refer to it as a hybrid long-term care plan.

Such policies are called asset-based because they are funded with your savings, home equity, retirement account, or various assets.

How Does Life Insurance-Based Long-Term Care Work?

With a life insurance policy, at the death of the insured, the company pays the death benefit to your beneficiaries.

The beneficiaries can use the death benefit to pay for funeral expenses, clear debts, or fulfill any financial needs.

With a hybrid life insurance plan, the death benefit can be used to pay for long-term care. So you have both life insurance and long-term care all in one plan.

This type of LTC insurance can help someone get over the thinking of what if I never need it?

Since none of us are immortal, even if you never need long-term care, you will likely need some life insurance when you die.

Plus, since you own the policy, you can sell your life insurance too.

How Does an Annuity-Based Long-Term Care Work?

Annuity-Based LTC insurance (LTCi) is my favorite type of Hybrid LTC Policy.

With the Annuity-Based Plan, you deposit a single premium into the policy, then the account value potentially triples for long-term care depending on your age when you purchase the annuity.

And because of the Pension Protection Act or PPA, along with the use of a 1035 exchange, she transferred her current taxable annuity and created a non-taxable flow of income to pay approximately $4,000 monthly for long-term care for up to 60 to 72 months.

You can also use your savings, IRA, 401K funds, or other assets to pay for the new LTCi annuity policy, here benefits are tax-free too.

See the diagram on the right. Mary, she is a 70-year-old female.

She had a current $100,000 annuity that she purchased over 12 years ago for $30,000. So it had a $70,000 "taxable" gain.

Using a 1035 exchange, she transferred her current taxable annuity and created a non-taxable flow of income to pay $4,000 monthly for long-term care for up to 72 months.

Pension Protection Act

$100,000

Creates

Approximately $300,000

$300,000

Creates $4,000 Per Month Tax-Free for Long-Term Care

Female age 70

With the single premium annuity, you must be healthy enough to qualify.

Remember that the qualification or underwriting requirements are less than that of traditional long-term care.

So even if you have been turned down for traditional LTCi, you may qualify for a hybrid annuity or life-insurance-based plan.

Who can help you purchase Long-Term Care Insurance?

It should be clear by now that long-term care insurance is quite different from other forms of insurance. It is much more complex.

Seek the help of a CLTC Insurance Professional. CLTCi stands for Certified in Long-Term Care Insurance Professional.

Long-term care insurance professionals with a CLTC designation do not focus on selling a product. Instead, they help create a comprehensive plan for your long-term care to protect your physical, financial, and emotional well-being.

Even though you think you'll never need long-term care, it's best to be prepared. See https://carefundingsolutions.com/ltc/

LTC Insurance Quote

Chapter Nine

LIFE SETTLEMENTS

A smart way to pay for long-term care is to use an in-force life insurance policy.

If you have a need for cash, selling your policy for cash could make a difference in the type of care and place you receive care.

Many of the nicer assisted living homes and communities require that the person moving in private pay for a period of time before they accept ALTCS. Money from a life insurance policy just might make the difference from an OK place to a wonderful place!

Generally, companies that purchase policies have a minimum face amount requirement that is $100,000. However, you may find a life settlement brokerage that will buy a smaller policy. The majority of the amount received is tax-free.

Once you sell your policy, you are no longer responsible for making the premiums on the policy.

SECTION III

WAYS TO PAY FOR LONG-TERM CARE

VETERANS' LONG-TERM CARE BENEFITS

THE

The Veteran Pension was previously called the Veterans Improved Pension with Aid and Attendance; in 2018, the Veterans Administration formally changed the name to Veterans Pension.

Here are the three "Ms" of "The 3 Ms to Veterans Pension Qualification."

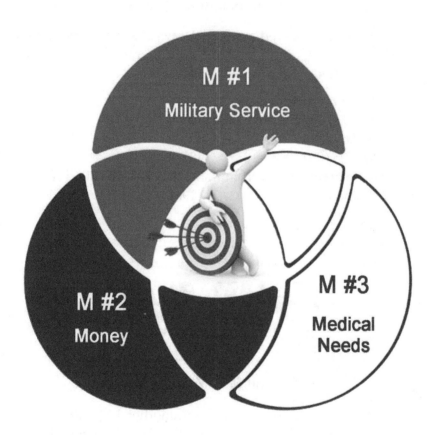

The First M is Military Service

A veteran must have served at least 90 days of active duty, with one day during a war period, and have an honorable discharge to be eligible for benefits.

The periods of war include:
World War II: 12/07/1941 to 12/31/1946
Korean War: 06/27/1950 to 01/31/1955
Vietnam War: 08/05/1964 to 05/07/1975*
*Veterans who actually served in the war zone, are called "boots on the ground," their start date is 02/28/1961

Gulf War: 08/02/1990 to present
Gulf War veterans must have two years of active duty to qualify; the two years are accumulative.

The Second M is Medical Need

A claimant must need assistance from another individual with at least two activities of daily living or ADLs: bathing, dressing, ambulating, toileting, transferring, and eating.

The VA considers medication management as an activity of daily living or ADL for someone with cognitive impairment.

Let's break down these ADLs and how the VA looks at them for qualification purposes.

Bathing: Unlike Medicaid/ALTCS with the Veterans Pension, assistance with bathing doesn't have to be someone physically hands-on bathing you. It can be stand-by assistance because you're a fall risk or need reminders to take a bath because you have Dementia.

Grooming: is also helpful for claims approval if noted by the Doctor completing the evaluation, VA form 21-2680.

Dressing: Like bathing, for dressing to qualify as an ADL, you don't have to have someone putting on and taking off your clothes. Someone with Dementia may need reminders to change their clothing, which will qualify as an ADL for the benefit.

Someone with arthritis may need help butting a button or tying a pair of shoes. All of these will qualify dressing as an ADL.

Ambulating or walking: Walking as an ADL has been on and off for Veterans Penson as a qualifier. I have had claims both approved and denied, with ambulating as one of the two ADL's.

Toileting: Toileting includes help getting down and up from the toilet. It's also help with personal hygiene, cleaning oneself, and incontinence care.

Transferring: Transferring is needing help getting up from a bed or chair to a wheelchair or help to a walker.

Eating: Eating can also be the need to be reminded to eat for someone with Dementia. They can be a choking risk and need their food cut up for them. Cooking is not an ADL.

Your Doctor's Role

The VA relies on your doctor's statement on the VA form 21- 2680.

If your doctor says you are a fall risk, you are a fall risk. If they say you have early onset of Dementia and you need medication management, then you need medication management, period.

The VA will not question your doctor's authority.

It is always best to have the doctor report reviewed by an Accredited Claims Agent before it is sent in to ensure it is completed properly before the VA receives it.

☀ VETERAN PENSION SECRET NUMBER ONE

Complete the doctor's report and ask the doctor to sign it. If they object, then give them a blank one and ask them to complete it.

They will take one look at the blank one and sign the other one.

Money = Income & Assets

The Third M is Money

What are the 2024 income and asset limits?

The VA calls this limit the "bright-line limit." From December 1, 2022 to November 30, 2024 the bright-line limit is $150,538. It is a combination of all household income and assets.

As mentioned, income is offset by unreimbursed medical expenses.

The limit changes on December 1 of each year. See our website for the current "bright-line Limit."

www. CareFundingSolutions.com/veterans/

Let's first define countable and non-countable income and assets.

Important to note the VA counts all marital household income and assets as jointly owned.

Income

Countable income includes: Social Security Income(s), all pension income, earned income from employment, interest income, RMD's from retirement accounts, short and long-term capital gains, and even gifts to you from your children to help pay for care is considered income. Payments from any source unless specifically excluded.

Income Limits: In order to qualify for the full pension benefit, your income must be less than your out-go for unreimbursed medical expenses and cost of care.

$$\backslash | \diagup$$

VETERAN PENSION SECRET
NUMBER TWO

There is not set income limits per se; this is because Unreimbursed Medical Expenses (UME) offset income.

So someone with a $7,500 per month income will qualify if they are spending $8,000 a month for unreimbursed medical care.

Deductible Medical Expenses: Unreimbursed medical expenses reduce countable income for purposes of increasing pension benefits. In order to be deducted from income, out-of-pocket, non-reimbursed medical expenses must exceed 5% of the VA Maximum Annual Pension Rate for the previous year.

Example 1: If you have a household income of $4,000 per month, and your cost of care in an assisted living community is $4,500 per month, you would have a monthly shortfall of $500. Therefore, you would qualify for the full monthly benefit.

Example 2: If your income is $4,500 per month, but your cost of care in an assisted living community is only $3,500 per month, you would have a $1,000 positive income.

Now, even though you have a $1,000 positive income, you would still qualify, but only for a partial benefit. The benefit amount paid is determined by subtracting the $1000 from the maximum benefit to get the partial benefit amount.

I have purposely simplified and left out parts of the income and out-go. The VA uses a more detailed MAPR equation than intended for this book.

Just understand there is not a set income limit per se. You need to spend your income on care in order to qualify for benefits.

See Maximum Annual Pension Rate or MAPR if you want a more detailed explanation. This can be found on our website, CareFundingSolutions.com.

THE CATCH 22

How do you pay for care to qualify for Veterans Pension if you don't have the Veterans Pension benefits to pay for care?

Classic Catch 22!

For some, this presents a real dilemma. How can they use all of their income to pay for care? They have food bills, housing, and utility bills to pay.

If they have savings, they can use the savings until the VA benefits are approved. Since it is a retroactive benefit paid back to the first of the month following the month the claim was submitted.

If you submit a claim on January 20, the benefits will accrue from February 1. So, once the lump sum benefits are paid, you can put it back in your savings.

But what if you have no savings? How do you pay for needed care if you don't have the money from the VA to pay for care?

This is less of a problem if you are in an assisted living home or community. The cost of assisted living is considered a medical expense. So you could consider moving from your home. Since an assisted living cost is all-inclusive, it includes room and board, utilities, food, and in some cases, cable.

So now you get the care and reduce your income with other expenses not otherwise included.

Another solution is to apply and get approved for a partial benefit, then once approved, dollar for dollar up to the maximum benefit

\\|/

that you spend on care will be paid and reimbursed by the VA.

VETERAN PENSION SECRET
NUMBER THREE

The cost of an assisted living community and group home is offset by income.

How much can you receive once approved?

Marital Status	Monthly	Annual
Single Veteran	$2,300	$27,600
Married Veteran	$2,727	$32,724
Spouse needs care	$1,685	$20,220
Surviving Spouse	$1,479	$17,748
Married both Spouses are Vets	$3,473	$41,676

The Total 2024 Veterans Pension with Aid and Attendance Benefits Amount

VA Benefits are TAX-FREE!

See www.CareFundingSolutions.com/Veterans for current rates.

Since the amount received is considered a benefit, not income, it is TAX-FREE and doesn't affect your Social Security benefits or taxes.

VETERAN PENSION SECRET
NUMBER FOUR

Finance the cost of care till your benefits come in, then use the back money or accrued benefits to pay off the loan. Some companies specialize in this type of financing; see our website for details.

Spouses of a Veteran often ask me if they can be paid to take care of my spouse.

I jokingly say, "You married him or her. Now you get to take care of them!"

The VA assumes you will provide care to the veteran at no charge since you are married.

VETERAN PENSION SECRET
NUMBER FIVE
A daughter / son, other family member or
friend can be a paid caregiver.

Surviving Spouse Qualification Requirements

First and foremost, understand the Veterans Pension is a veteran's benefit, and to be eligible as a surviving spouse, you must have been married to the veteran at the time of their death and not remarried.

The "D" in Divorce = Denied. If you divorced the veteran, you are not eligible.

Marriage under VA rules: Must be married for at least one year prior to death.

The VA does allow for common-law marriages if the veteran lived in states that recognized common-law marriages. These are

Colorado, Iowa, Kansas, Montana, New Hampshire, Oklahoma, Rhode Island, South Carolina, Texas, and Utah. Also, the District of Columbia.

VETERAN PENSION SECRET NUMBER SIX

A surviving spouse can continue to pursue a
claim for her deceased husband and receive the
accrued benefits postmortem.

Also, if the spouse develops the need for extended care, the date of claim is the veteran's date of death for the surviving spouse.

This date is held for up to one year from the date of death.

VETERAN PENSION SECRET NUMBER SEVEN

The Veterans Pension can be used for
Home Care and Home Health Care services.

Just keep the income out-go ratio in mind to determine how many hours of care you will need to reduce your income to qualify for the full benefit.

VETERAN PENSION SECRET NUMBER EIGHT

Someone on hospice can get their claim expedited.

Send proof to the pension center along with your claim or update your claim and the VA is required to expedite the process.

HOW TO FILE A VETERANS PENSION CLAIM?

I will never forget this; I was at the VA Regional Office on Central Avenue in Phoenix, AZ. I would often go there at the end of each month to get my veteran "Intent to File a Claim" form 21-0966 officially date stamped.

A woman came to the counter while I was waiting for the person to help me. She said, "I'm the daughter of a Vietnam Veteran and have been elected by my siblings to help get my father's Veteran's Pension claim filed; I have no idea what forms are needed or what to do."

The VA employee turned and walked to the forms cabinet and said; As she reached for the form, "I **think** you will need this one. And I **think** you will need this one, and I **think** you will need this one."

I knew the lady assisting her by her first name and often enjoyed seeing her. She was so friendly and genuine, and she would even give me a friendly hug when I got there. It was all I could do to keep my mouth shut. I wanted to say; "What do you mean you "**THINK!**" You're with the VA!"

I didn't want to embarrass her or make any comments. But in my mind I thought, **"YOU THINK?** What do you mean YOU THINK you need this one!"

How long does it take to get a claim approved?

Due to changes in the past 12 months with resources at the Veterans Administration, a claim can take eight to ten months to be approved.

Done wrong, a claim can take a year or longer to complete or even be denied.

As the receptionist at the VA said, "I think you need this form."

Let me just say, **"I THINK"** you should consider seeking the help of an Accredited Claims Agent.

∖∣⁄
VETERAN PENSION SECRET
NUMBER NINE

Only those recognized by the Secretary of Veterans Affairs can "legally" help a Veteran with a VA claim.

Myth: A common myth about VA Pension Benefits is that anyone can help a veteran with a claim.

I often learn about unauthorized people who make unsuitable recommendations while helping veterans with the claims process. These individuals are **breaking the law.**

Fact: The law says that anyone can help a veteran with **one claim, one time.** Helping someone "one time" can be misunderstood.

Title 38 CFR § 14.630 (a) states that any person may be authorized to prepare, present, and prosecute one claim.

This allows a family member or friend to help a veteran with a claim, **one time**.

This is clarified under Title 38 USC § 5901:

"Except as provided by section 5901 of Title 38, no individual may act as an agent or attorney in the preparation, presentation, or prosecution of any claim under laws administered by the Secretary unless such individual has been recognized for such purposes by the Secretary."

These are the people recognized by the Secretary.

- **VA Accredited Claims Agents**,**
- **VA Accredited Attorneys,**
- **Veteran Service Officers**

Notice who is not on the list that the Secretary of Veterans Affairs recognizes:

The VA added to the explanation in their Fast Letter 06-26: **"Representation before VA consists of actions associated with the preparation, presentation, or prosecution of claim for a VA claimant ... Among other things, representation includes counseling on veterans benefits, gathering information necessary to file a claim for benefits, preparing claim forms ..."**

This is violated by many well-meaning advisors, particularly those who are counseling on VA benefits and gathering information. Advisors cross the line as soon as they go from providing general education on VA benefits to answering specific questions.

Questions include whether a veteran will qualify based on their current medical needs, wartime military service, or if they have too many assets. This is a violation of the intent and spirit of the law.

I call these individuals that are knowingly violating the law "VA Pirates." Beware of these individuals; someone willing to break the law with this matter, what else are they willing to do?

If you are a health care professional, home health provider, assisted living community or group homeowner or director, or senior placement agent. Be sure that the VA recognizes the person you are referring to is an Accredited Claims Agent, Veteran Service Officer, or VA Accredited Attorney.

If you want to see if the Secretary of Veterans Affairs authorizes the person you are working with to help veterans, see:
https://www.va.gov/ogc/apps/accreditation/

Ask the person helping you if they are VA accredited.
Better yet, check for yourself here:

On the first screen, you will see three radio buttons:
⊙Attorney ⊙ Claims Agent ⊙ VSO Representative

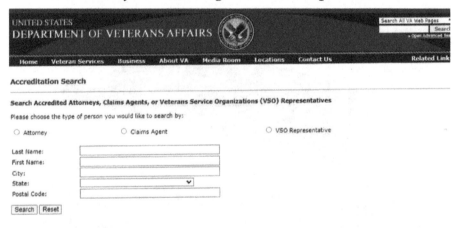

If, you choose ⊙ Claims Agent and then under the name you type "**Dabbs**," you will see this screen.

There you will see if the person you put in the last and first name box or just last name comes up, showing they are approved. If you put the last name, "Dabbs, " you will see this when you click on the person's name:

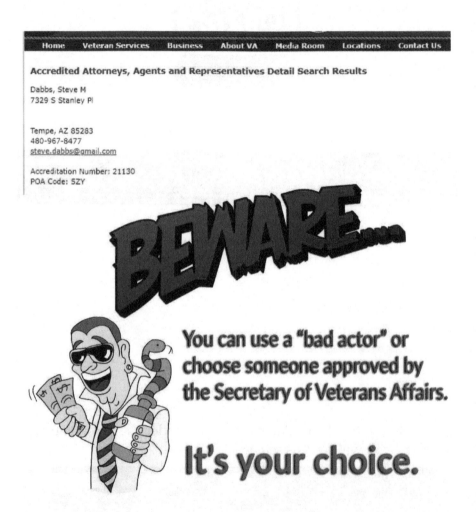

∿

VETERAN PENSION SECRET
NUMBER TEN

Independent living communities "can" be used as an Unreimbursed Medical Expense - UME.

Many believe this is not true.

I have prepared hundreds of claims for Veterans that were living in independent communities.

The key here is you have to have the need for the assistance of another individual with at least two activities of daily living and be paying for needed care, which is the same that is required for an Assisted Living Community.

Lastly, the Independent Community must provide 24/7 staffing and be considered a safe and secure environment.

Veterans Directive Care Program

The Home Care Program is a community-based program. For both wartime veterans and non-wartime veterans. It will provide service in the home for activities of daily living. These are:

Bathing, dressing, medication reminders, transportation, meal preparation, transferring, personal care, respite care, light housekeeping, laundry, and companionship.

Veteran-Directed care is for veterans who need assistance with activities of daily living (e.g., bathing and getting dressed) or

instrumental activities of daily living (e.g., fixing meals); are isolated, or their caregiver is experiencing burden.

This program is based on funding and availability in specific counties. Like the Home Care Benefits, it is managed through the VA Medical Centers.

Long-Term Care Planning
can preserve assets and
Protect your Nest Egg.

SECTION IV

WHAT IS ALTCS?

What is ALTCS? (Video)

Chapter Ten

ALTCS INTRODUCTION

Arizona's Medicaid Long-Term Care System, or ALTCS, is the nation's financial safety for long-term care.

Medicaid is a state and federally-funded program that is administered by each state individually.

Medicaid is the primary payer for long-term care services paying for over 40% of people in America that need long-term care.

ALTCS is an acronym for Arizona Long Term Care System. It's pronounced All-Tex or All-Techs.

Sometimes referred to as "Arizona's Long-Term Care for "Seniors."

In Arizona, the state agency that administers the Medicaid program is Arizona Health Care Cost Containment System (AHCCCS).

ALTCS SECRET
NUMBER ONE

Medicaid is Long-Term Care Insurance.

The insurance premiums for the program are paid for with your tax dollars.

Those who are wise plan can preserve assets and still have Medicaid/ ALTCS pay for future long-term care.

Even those that need care now, with the help of a Certified Medicaid Planner, can help design a plan that will protect assets and still allow someone to receive benefits under the program.

Chapter Eleven

IS ALTCS PLANNING BOTH LEGAL AND ETHICAL?

Is Medicaid Planning Legal?

The Courts have answered the question of whether or not ALTCS / Medicaid planning is legal. The answer is yes; it's 100% legal.

In a landmark case, Helvering (Commissioner of the IRS v. Gregory (1934) Judge Learned Hand stated, in the Helvering v. Gregory case, that, "Anyone may so arrange his affairs that his taxes shall be as low as possible; he is not bound to choose that pattern which will best pay the Treasury, there is not even a patriotic duty to increase one's taxes."

The US Supreme Court went on to uphold this decision: see Gregory v. Helvering, 293 US at 468-470

In 1996 Congress added a provision under the "Health Insurance Portability and Accountability Act of 1996."

For a very brief moment, Congress attempted to make Medicaid planning illegal.

The law was dubbed the "Granny Goes to Jail Law."

Violators of the law were subject to fines of up to $25,000 or imprisonment for up to 5 years or both. Section 217 of the law made it a crime to: "knowingly and willfully disposes of assets (including by any transfer in trust) for an individual to become eligible for medical assistance under a State plan under title XIX if disposing of the assets results in the imposition of a period of ineligibility for such assistance under section 1917(c),"

Then shortly after the law went into effect, in September of 1998, the New York State Bar Association sued the Justice Department and was ruled that the law violated the First Amendment.

Before the Judgement was handed down, then-Attorney General Janet Reno determined that the law was unconstitutional because it violated the First Amendment. She told Congress that the Justice Department would not enforce the law.

Just like state and federal income tax planning is allowed, Medicaid- ALTCS Planning is permitted.

Now, not reporting income is illegal. Just like hiding money and filing a fraudulent Medicaid claim is ILLEGAL, too.

On the other hand, converting assets from a countable to a non-countable asset is not.

Is Medicaid-ALTCS Planning Ethical?

How is preserving assets for a spouse or loved one unethical?

Is leaving a gift to a church or synagogue somehow wrong?

How is providing funding for a college education for a grandchild unethical?

Why is using the tax dollars you paid over your lifetime to help you pay for long-term care unethical?

Remember "My Why" at the beginning of this book? I told you the story about the lady who only has $25,000 to live on for the rest of her life.

I dare you to tell her it's unethical to do VA and Medicaid Planning.

Regardless of whether you need care now or are worried you may need care in the future, the time to start Medicaid Planning is now.

Chapter Twelve

GIFTING IS NOT ILLEGAL!

I was conducting an ALTCS financial interview with a state caseworker, and the financial caseworker asked the series of questions they always do.

Here is the question I love the most. "Has the person applying gifted any money in the last five years?" I love to say, **"Yes, they did. I told them to so I could file the claim."**

At that moment, the ALTCS worker blurted out, *"That's illegal!"*

I responded with this: "Oh my God. I tell people to do that all the time, I am going to go to jail!" Then I said, "You know that it isn't illegal."

She said, "Well, **no**, but it causes a penalty."

I responded, "But you just said it was illegal! Yet you know it isn't."

I told her my concern is if you say that to someone I am helping and now doubts my ethics or knowledge to help them with their claim.

I went on to say, "You have no business saying such a thing to anyone."

So, what is the penalty? It is a time penalty. One that you can calculate into the application approval process.

I call the penalty a blessing because the gift allows someone to apply for benefits and still have assets to pay for unreimbursed medical care in the future.

Combining the gift with a Medicaid Compliant Annuity allows some to reduce the penalty period and have the funds to pay for care during the penalty period. See Chapter Fifteen.

Watch this short video to get a better understanding of the "Gifting Strategy."

Chapter Thirteen

THE ALTCS ELIGIBILITY AND QUALIFICATION REQUIREMENTS

What are the ALTCS Eligibility and Qualification Requirements?

You can be "Eligible" and still not be "Qualified."

Eligibility Requirements:

In addition to meeting the financial and medical requirements, the applicant must also meet the following:

1. Be a US citizen or qualified immigrant.
2. Have a Social Security number or applied for one.
3. Be an Arizona resident (See ALTCS Secret #2).
4. Age (65 or older or under 18), blind, or disabled.
5. Must apply for other potential benefits (Veterans Pension)
6. Live in a Medicaid-approved living arrangement

ALTCS SECRET
NUMBER TWO

You're considered a resident of Arizona, the minute you arrive in the state as long as you intend to stay in Arizona!

I have helped many people move from other states. They are considered an Arizona resident when they arrive, as they intend to stay here permanently. Many even start the application process before they are physically in Arizona.

This can be confusing because the Arizona Department of Revenue doesn't consider you a resident until you have lived in the state for nine months in a calendar year.

Financial and Medical Requirements

The ALTCS qualification requirements are divided into two parts, these are:

- Medical and the need for long-term care services
- Financial requirements

Note that you can be qualified for medical coverage but still not be eligible for long-term care services. Meaning you could be financially eligible for Arizona Medicaid benefits and not have a high enough medical need (nursing level) to qualify for long-term care benefits. Or you may be medically qualified but not meet the financial eligibility requirements.

"An applicant must be qualified medically and financially to be approved for insurance benefits."

The Medical Qualification Requirements

The ALTCS medical assessment process starts with an ALTCS medical assessor, generally a registered nurse or a social worker, who conducts an interview and reviews current medical records.

ALTCS uses a 60-point score to determine an applicant's ALTCS medical eligibility.

An applicant must be at a nursing level of care.

The assessment process is called a Pre-Admission Screening or PAS—the PAS takes about an hour. Because of COVID, the PAS is now conducted over the phone rather than in person. However, you can request an in-person visit if you wish.

The PAS Scoring process is based on Medical and Functional needs. It is essential to understand that PAS Medical Assessment **is a "subjective process."**

Therein lies the problem with the PAS assessment process. Unlike the Veterans Pension, ALTCS is somewhat subjective. The VA relies solely on what your doctor states in the "VA Physicians"

Evaluation Report the "VA Form 21-2680. With the VA, if your doctor says you need care, you need care, **period.**

With ALTCS, it is based primarily on the ALTCS Medical assessor's evaluation and opinion. And the Medical assessor can deny the application. **The good news is you can appeal the decision.**

Your Certified Medicaid Planner can help by coaching you so you can answer the questions correctly. And can assist in the appeal process too.

ALTCS SECRET
NUMBER THREE

Don't lie about your health during the process, but don't brag about your health either. The doctor, hospital, and rehab records will be used to support the assessment done by ALTCS to be approved.

The PAS Scoring Process

In Exhibit One on the next page, note the three categories on the right. Rating, Weight, and Score.

The Rating is a maximum score of three (3) or 20 points, except for Neurocognitive Disorder, where the maximum score is one (1) or 20 points.

Take someone with Dementia; they might be able to take a bath but may need reminders to wash everywhere and use soap. They might only get a weighted score of one out of three (1 times 5) or five points.

At the same time, someone who needs someone to bathe them hands-on, washing their body, hair and private parts would have a weighted score of three or a maximum of fifteen available for bathing.

Sample PAS Assessment

Functional Score	Rating	Weight	Score
Mobility	1	5	5
Transferring	0	5	0
Bathing	3	5	15
Dressing	1	5	5
Grooming	2	5	10
Eating	0	5	0
Toileting	1	5	5
Activities of Daily Living (ADL's Subtotal)			40
Bowel Continence	0	1	0
Blader Continence	0	1	0
Continence Subtotal:			0
Vision	0	2	0
Communication/Sensory Subtotal:			0
Immediate Environment	0	0.5	0
Place of Residence	0	0.5	0
City	0	0.5	0
State	0	0.5	0
Time of Day	0	0.5	0
Day	0	0.5	0
Month	2	0.5	1
Year	2	0.5	1
Orientation- Place Subtotal:			2
Wandering - Frequency	0	1.5	0
Wandering - Intervention	0	1.5	0
Self Injurious Behavior - Frequency	0	1.5	0
Self Injurious Behavior - Intervention	0	1.5	0
Aggression - Frequency	0	1.5	0
Aggression - Intervention	0	1.5	0
Resistiveness - Frequency	0	1.5	0
Resistiveness - Intervention	0	1.5	0
Disruptive Behavior - Frequency	0	1.5	0
Disruptive Behavior - Intervention	0	1.5	0
Behaviors Subtotal:			0
Functional Subtotal:			42
Neurocognitive Disorder	2	10	20
Neurological Subtotal			20
Summary:			
Functional Subtotal:			42
Medical Subtotal:			20
TOTAL SCORE:			62

See the total score of 62 points that is enough to qualify for benefits. Each state uses a similar scoring technique to determine if the person is eligible. This is the method that the State of Arizona uses.

Financial Qualification Requirements

Like the Veterans Pension, the financial requirements have both income limits or caps and asset limits.

The Income Cap

Arizona is one of 23 states referred to as "Income Cap States." For 2024 the income cap for a single applicant is $2,829 per month of countable income. This changes annually, so be sure to check our website for current income caps. www.CareFundingSolutions.com

A handful of income sources are not considered countable, like the Aid and the Attendance portion of the Veteran's Pension, which is not countable. VA Pension is a tax-free benefit, not income.

So, if your income is below the cap and you get approved for Veterans Pension with Aid and Attendance, not only does only the A&A portion not count as income, but you are allowed to keep it along with your "Personal Needs Allowance.

This can present a problem because you must spend it each month so that your assets do not exceed the asset cap of $2000.

The ALTCS application will be denied even if income is even one dollar above the cap. The same is true if your assets exceed the limit.

If an applicant's income is above the cap, qualification is still possible with an Income Only Trust -IOT a.k.a. "Miller Trust."

This "Income Only Trust" is flow-through. Income is assigned to the trust, and then income is used to pay the share of the cost of care minus allowable expenses and the Personal Needs Allowance.

The IOT is a carefully prepared document by either a Certified Legal Document Preparer or an attorney.

"Note, You do not need an elder law attorney to help with Medicaid Planning."

Income Caps are updated on January 1 of each year. See our website, CareFundingSolutions.com, for current caps.

See CareFundingSolutions.com/altcs-income-only-trust/

ALTCS SECRET
NUMBER FOUR

All assets are considered jointly owned by married couples, and all income is separate.

The non-applicant or at-home spouse, technically called the non-institutional spouse, can have unlimited income.

Meaning the non-institutional spouse does not have a cap or maximum, whereas the applicant does. And the non-institutional spouse does not have any financial responsibility to use their income to pay for their spouse's care.

Noting that unlimited means just that, "unlimited." The well spouse can have $150,000 monthly income, and their spouse will still qualify.

2024 Married Couple Income Calculations

The rule is relatively straightforward with a single applicant.

Whereas with a married couple, it can be much more complicated.

The first rule is that there is no need to use an Income Only Trust for a married couple with an income less than double the income cap of $2,742 or $5,484 per month.

To add to the confusion as already mentioned, a spouse not on ALTCS can have unlimited income.

Married Income Example #1

Mary and Bob have been married for 42 years, and Bob has a modest pension and Social Security that totals $3,201 per month. Mary only has Social Security of $1,345 per month. Their combined income is $4,546, less than the $5,484 per month, so there is no need for an "Income Only Trust."

Married Income Example #2

Jackie and Bill recently married, and shortly after they were married, Jackie developed Dementia. Bill cared for her for several years until he could no longer provide care.

Looking for funding to pay for needed Care, Bill applied for ALTCS.

Mary's income is above the income cap, and Bill's income is over

$4000 per month. So, the household income total is over the combined total of $5,046.

So, Jackie will need an "Income Only Trust" to qualify.

Here, Jackie's income will be used for care, minus her Personal Needs Allowance and other allowable expenses, and Bill will be able to keep 100% of his income.

ALTCS SECRET
NUMBER FIVE

A spouse can get part of the applicant's spouse's income to help with their living expenses.

The Medicaid Spousal Impoverishment provisions allow for a certain amount of the couple's combined income to be protected for the spouse living in the community.

This allowance is called the Minimum Monthly Maintenance Needs Allowance, Shelter Standard, and Standard Utility Allowance (MMMNA).

For example, if the non-applicant spouse's income is low, say $1,300 per month, and the applicant spouse's income is over the limit and an "Income Only Trust" was needed, say $3,200 per month, the non- applicant spouse can get the MMMNA, housing and utility allowance.

The Spouse's Minimum Monthly Maintenance Needs Allowance (MMMNA)

The Minimum Monthly Maintenance Needs Allowance (MMMNA) is the minimum monthly income the non-applicant or at-home spouse is allowed to have.

The non-applicant or at-home spouse is also given allowances for housing and utilities. These are combined with the MMMNA, which is $2,555 for 2024.

These additional allowances are called the Shelter Standard and the Standard Utility Allowance. Here are the 2024 amounts:

Shelter Standard: $740.00
Standard Utility Allowance: $318.00
See the carefundingsolutions.com website for current figures.

Maximum Monthly Maintenance Needs Allowance, the Shelter Standard and the Standard Utility Allowance are combined with the MMMNA; these three allowances create the Maximum Monthly Maintenance Needs Allowance, which is currently $3,715.

HIDING ASSETS TO QUALIFY – THIS IS A TERRIBLE IDEA!

Why Hiding Assets to Qualify is a Terrible Idea!

Don't try to Hide Assets!

Hiding assets to qualify for Medicaid/ALTCS is illegal. This is called Medicaid Fraud. The AHCCCS Inspector General oversees the program to reduce fraud, waste, and abuse of the program.

The Arizona Revised Statute (ARS 36-2918.01) states all contractors, providers, and non-providers shall advise the (AHCCCS) Director or his designee immediately in writing of any cases of suspected fraud or abuse.

Medicaid fraud, if convicted, can result in jail time, probation, community service, and fines, and you may have to pay back the benefits received.

Medicaid/ALTCS planning is not hiding assets. It is a legal way to reduce countable assets or convert them to non-countable assets in order to qualify for benefits.

Again, hiding assets to qualify is against the law.

Medicaid/ALTCS planning is not!

Without planning, when you run out of money or "Spend-Down," you do not have any money left to pay for anything, you are broke.

ALTCS SECRET
NUMBER SIX

It is **"not illegal"** for a family member to pay the difference between what ALTCS pays and the retail rate (what you pay) with money preserved through ALTCS Planning.

By utilizing the strategies described in this book, you can preserve assets and then agree with the care home to pay the difference between what ALTCS pays and the normal private pay rate.

Larger corporately owned communities are less likely to agree to this as a strategy, but most group care homes will be happy to have such an arrangement.

If hired, I will meet with the assisted living owners or managers and help them understand this payment strategy.

By the way, this is true for in-home care, too, and you can pay the difference to get better-qualified home care providers into your home to care for you.

ALTCS SECRET
NUMBER SEVEN

"KEEP CALM AND CONVERT"

I often say; "Keep Calm and Convert."

Convert Countable assets to non-countable assets and apply for ALTCS.

So here is a short list of conversion options.

- Pay off your mortgage or make home improvements
- Buy a vehicle
- Buy needed personal items
- Pay off secure debt
- Set up a formal gifting plan
- Buy a Medicaid Compliant Annuity
- **Pre-pay final expenses with a Funeral Trust**

Chapter Fourteen

ALTCS HOME AND COMMUNITY-BASED SERVICES

Arizona is an approved Home and Community-Based Services State or HCBS waiver state, and under the HCBS program, benefits extend and include:

- Home Daycare
- Personal and respite care
- Medical Transportation
- Mental health services
- Homemaker services
- Home care and home health aides.

It's important to understand that the ALTCS qualification requirements are precisely the same whether you stay in your home, a certified ALTCS community, or a group home.

The difference between being in a community or group home is the way care services are provided and how they treat the applicant's income.

Through the HCBS waiver program, an applicant can receive care in their home and have a family caregiver, including their spouse, be a paid caregiver.

Scan the above and watch this short video and learn about ALTCS home care.

Chapter Fifteen

MEDICAID COMPLIANT ANNUITIES – HOW THEY HELP QUALIFY FOR ALTCS

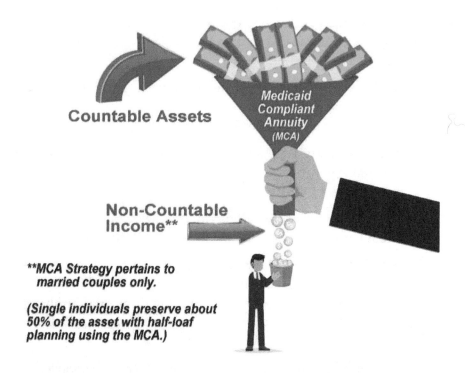

Countable Assets

Medicaid
Compliant
Annuity
(MCA)

**Non-Countable
Income****

***MCA Strategy pertains to
married couples only.*

*(Single individuals preserve about
50% of the asset with half-loaf
planning using the MCA.)*

A Medicaid Compliant Annuity (MCA) is a Single Premium Immediate Annuity or SPIA. *(pronounced "speee-ah")*

The Medicaid Compliant Annuity, Single Premium Immediate Annuity, has only one real purpose. It is to convert countable assets into non-countable income to qualify for Medicaid long-term care.

Requirements of a Medicaid-Compliant Annuity

This amazing financial tool commonly used in Medicaid planning converts your countable assets into a non-countable income stream.

But not all annuities are Medicaid-compliant.

The Deficit Reduction Act of 2005 set the guidelines for an annuity to become "Medicaid Compliant." Medicaid annuities must abide by these guidelines to be considered a non-countable asset.

1. **The annuity must be irrevocable:** The parties, terms, and payment amount of the Medicaid Compliant Annuity cannot be altered or revoked.

2. **The annuity must be non-assignable:** The parties to the annuity contract cannot sell it in the secondary market or assign (or transfer) to another person.

3. **Fixed annuity term rule:** The duration of the annuity and income payout term must be equal to or less than the life expectancy of the owner.

4. **No balloon or deferral payments:** The annuity payments must be equally distributed monthly to the annuity owner.

5. **The State Medicaid Agency must be made the beneficiary:** The annuity contract must name the state Medicaid agency Arizona Health Care Cost Containment System (AHCCCS) as the primary beneficiary, equal to the amount spent as benefits on the Medicaid recipient.

   If married, the spouse is the primary beneficiary, and AHCCCS is contingent.

How is a Medicaid Compliant Annuity used to qualify for Medicaid in Arizona?

Let's explore a few examples of how the Medicaid Compliant Annuity works to help you qualify.

Example One: A Case for a Married Couple to consider a Medicaid-Compliant Annuity.

Take Mike and Maureen. They have countable assets of $308,280.

Mike has advanced Dementia and needs to be in a memory care facility or directive care home for the cognitively impaired.

Mike's income is $1850 per month, and Maureen has a pension and Social Security of $3,400 per month. So, they have a combined income of $5,250 per month.

The average cost for the care facility is $6,000 per month.

Maureen needs about $4,000 a month minimum to live on and realizes they will deplete their retirement savings will be depleted in 57 months!

How can the MCA Annuity help change this outcome? How does the MCA help by leaving the non-institutional spouse destitute and paying for her husband's care? Keep reading.

Medicaid/ALTCS Spend-Down

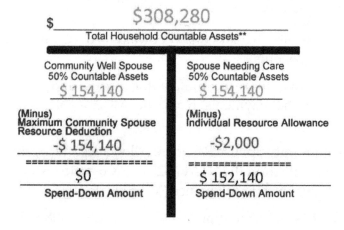

As you can see, the non-institutional spouse or community spouse is allowed to keep $154,140 (on the left of bar in the center) and the spouse needing care is $2,000, so the spend down required to qualify is $152,140.

Now they take the $154,140 and purchase a 48-month MCA.

The Medicaid Compliant Annuity - MCA will produce an exempt income of approximately $3222, paid to the non-institutional spouse.

An MCA annuity can also be purchased for a shorter period of time. A 6-month payout would generate a $26,244 monthly income and end in 6 months.

This can be advantageous if that asset is not qualified or IRA/401K funds. Consult with a Certified Medicaid Planner; remember, the well spouse can have unlimited income.

The Six Months Annuity Option

The $152,140 countable asset is used to purchase the MCA and the income is considered non-countable or exempt.

The income that the MCA produces is approximately $25,445 per month for six months.

Now, Mike applies for Arizona Medicaid - ALTCS benefits and is approved for benefits.

Maureen is able to reaccumulate the assets and now has the $154,140 and the payments from the MCA – SPIA total assets preserved:

- Community Spouse Resource Allowance =$154,140
- Payments from the MCA ($25,455 X 6 = $152,672)
- Personal Needs Allowance (Mike's) = $ 2,000

    Total assets after approval............... = $ 308,812

Subtract Medicaid Compliant Annuity fees = -$ 6,564

Total assets preserved = $302,247

(**Disclaimer there are essential steps that must be taken. These steps must be done in the proper order for this strategy to be successful.")

This is not a do-it-yourself project.

Consult a Certified Medicaid Planner™ who fully understands this strategy and the proper order of the steps in the process.

For Single Applicants Needing Extended Care

Qualifying as a single individual is more of a challenge because they cannot shift assets to a non-institutional spouse. So, they must do what is referred to as (modern) half-loaf planning.

Single Applicant Example: A case for someone single to purchase a Medicaid Compliant Annuity (MCA) to qualify for Arizona Medicaid.

Take Bob. He recently lost his wife, Joan, of 50 years, due to complications with Dementia.

Now Bob has about $120,000 left to his name.

He needs care but does not want to spend all his assets on long-term care, he would like to leave some money to his niece who both he and his wife love dearly.

Here is what the CMP helps Bob do.

Bob uses $42,000 to buy a new car so that his niece can use it to pick him up and take him to lunch, the doctor, and family events. He puts his niece on the insurance as a non-owner driver.

The car is an exempt asset, and the State of Arizona AHCCCS does not make any recovery on it when Bob passes (Meaning the state does not make an heir sell the vehicle and reimburse what they paid for Bob's extended care costs).

Now the $42,000 countable asset becomes a non-countable asset – a vehicle. This reduces Bob's countable assets, the $120,000, to $78,000. ($120,000 - $42,000= $78,000)

Bob buys a Funeral Trust to pre-pay his final burial expenses. He only sets just enough to pay for the final costs, which he and his niece figure would be about $5,500.

This purchase of the Funeral Trust reduced Bob's countable assets from $78,000 to $72,500. ($78,000 - $5,500 = $72,500)

Still, $70,500 is over the current 2024 Arizona Medicaid asset limit. Step Three: Bob gifts $50,000 to his niece.

Funny thing, when Bob told the executive director that he was going to gift $50,000 to his niece so he could qualify for Medicaid, she told him, "That's illegal!"

It's not! It only causes a period of ineligibility, that's all.

Arizona Medicaid uses what is called a Divestment Penalty Divisor, which is used to calculate the period of ineligibility that is caused by a gift.

The current 2024 Arizona Medicaid Penalty Divisor is $7,867.16 in Maricopa County and $7,281 in all other counties. (See the website for the current amount.)

Here, the gift from Bob of $50,000 to his niece will cause a little over a six-month period of time that Bob would be ineligible for Arizona Medicaid benefits.

($50,000 ÷ $7867. = 6.36 or 6.36 months)

Now that leaves only $20,500 left to spend to be qualified for Arizona Medicaid. ($70,500 - $50,000 = $20,500)

After the CMP fee for planning and application assistance and the setup fee for the Medicaid Compliant Annuity.

(Call for fees and details at 800-543- 0530)

This leaves $17,000 to purchase a Medicaid Compliant Annuity for a 6-month period, generating about $2,840 per month for the six months.

Which is just short of what is needed to pay through the ineligibility period because of the $50,000.

Bob now has $2000 in countable assets and can apply and be approved for Arizona Medicaid long-term care.

Summary of the single plan discussed.

Bob and Joan could have started a plan and preserved much of their assets from the sale of their home had they been given the correct information about Arizona Medicaid, as you saw in example one.

Once Joan died, Bob's niece contacted the CMPs at Care Funding Solutions for help.

**Disclaimer, there are essential steps that must be taken. These steps must be done in the proper order for this strategy to be successful.

This again is not a Do-it-Yourself project. Consult a Certified Medicaid Planner who fully understands this strategy and the steps needed.)

(See *Gifting is not illegal* video link: **tinyurl.com/Giftingisnotillegal**

How to Set Up a Medicaid Compliant Annuity?

Given the highly technical nature of Arizona Medicaid Planning, anyone interested in pursuing an Arizona Medicaid qualification strategy using a Medicaid Compliant Annuity should seek the guidance of a professional Certified Medicaid Planner (CMP).

Chapter Sixteen

IMPORTANT LEGAL DOCUMENTS NEEDED FOR LONG-TERM CARE PLANNING

The Estate Plan and Long-Term Care Planning Documents Checklist

- **Will and Testament**

A Will is your declaration of intent on how to distribute your property after your death.

The problem with only having a will is that it's a <u>guaranteed</u> ticket to probate.

- **Trusts**

Unlike a Will, the trust doesn't go to Probate Court to be settled.

A Trust is an arrangement that offers incredible flexibility for you to manage assets (fully or partially) to achieve certain objectives.

In a Trust, the trust becomes the property's owner and trustee the property's manager. With a living trust the grantor (you) and the trustee can be the same.

- ## Durable Power of Attorney

The Durable Power of Attorney allows you to appoint an Agent or Proxy who would manage your properties, fulfill your financial responsibilities, and make decisions regarding your financial affairs.

The Agent will act on your behalf and make decisions when you can't do it yourself due to physical or mental incapacitation.

- ## Beneficiary Designations

Assets with a named beneficiary skip the probate process, thereby reaching the intended beneficiary directly after your death.

To keep your assets outside probate, you must name a beneficiary during your lifetime.

Naming a beneficiary can be a trust or will substitute.

Advanced Healthcare Power of Attorney

Like the DPOA, a Healthcare Power of Attorney is a document that provides instructions on medical care if you're not in a position to make those decisions yourself.

The Healthcare Power of Attorney has two parts:

Living Will: In the event of incapacity, the Living Will provides answers to questions on treatment options, medications, end-of-life care, etc.

Healthcare Power of Attorney: An agent would be appointed who is responsible for making crucial medical decisions if you're unconscious, in a coma, or become mentally unstable.

Chapter Seventeen

MY FINAL WORDS

Helping those with both non-crisis and crisis long-term care planning and assisting veterans with the Veterans Pension and Arizona Medicaid benefits over the past 19-plus years has been the most fulfilling aspect of my financial planning career.

As you can now see, finding and paying for the proper long-term care can be a daunting and challenging task.

It is essential to seek the help of professionals like a Certified Medicaid Planner™, a Certified Document Preparer, a VA-Accredited Claims Agent, and a Certified Placement and Referral Specialist. Trying to do this on your own can be a costly mistake.

Thank you very much for buying and reading my book!

Please give the book to someone you know that might benefit from the information.

Also call me office at 480-967-8477 if you would like me to send the book to someone that might benefit from it.

And lastly, I have a one-hour presentation that I will do at no charge for groups of twenty or more individuals. Call to set up a meeting at your church, club, or association. I will happily provide this book and my newest book, *Medicaid For Millionaires, and Everyone Else.*

SCAN ME

REFERENCES MATERIAL & SOURCES

Contact
Steve Dabbs
480-967-8477
info@carefundingsolutions.com

Get a Free
Long-Term &
Short Term Care
Insurance Quote

Legal Documents
for
Long-Term Care
Planning

Free Phone Consultation with CMP Steve Dabbs

Michael Anthony, JD, CMP™ | the Author of "The Medicaid Planning Guidebook,"

"The Arizona Medicaid and Veterans Pension Guide" 2024 edition
"Medicaid for Millionaires" 2024 edition
Certification for Long-Term Care – Reference and training material

https://www.medicaid.gov/
42 U.S Code § 1320 – 1396
https://VA.gov
Title 38 of the U.S. Code
Adjudication Procedure Manual Department of Veterans Affairs
Photos and Illustrations purchased from IstockPhotos.com

Made in the USA
Las Vegas, NV
30 September 2024